S. Hrg. 113–135

COUNTERTERRORISM POLICIES AND PRIORITIES: ADDRESSING THE EVOLVING THREAT

HEARING

BEFORE THE

COMMITTEE ON FOREIGN RELATIONS UNITED STATES SENATE

ONE HUNDRED THIRTEENTH CONGRESS

FIRST SESSION

MARCH 20, 2013

Printed for the use of the Committee on Foreign Relations

Available via the World Wide Web: http://www.gpo.gov/fdsys/

U.S. GOVERNMENT PRINTING OFFICE
WASHINGTON : 2014

86–146 PDF

For sale by the Superintendent of Documents, U.S. Government Printing Office
Internet: bookstore.gpo.gov   Phone: toll free (866) 512–1800; DC area (202) 512–1800
Fax: (202) 512–2104   Mail: Stop IDCC, Washington, DC 20402–0001

COMMITTEE ON FOREIGN RELATIONS

ROBERT MENENDEZ, New Jersey, *Chairman*

BARBARA BOXER, California	BOB CORKER, Tennessee
BENJAMIN L. CARDIN, Maryland	JAMES E. RISCH, Idaho
ROBERT P. CASEY, Jr., Pennsylvania	MARCO RUBIO, Florida
JEANNE SHAHEEN, New Hampshire	RON JOHNSON, Wisconsin
CHRISTOPHER A. COONS, Delaware	JEFF FLAKE, Arizona
RICHARD J. DURBIN, Illinois	JOHN McCAIN, Arizona
TOM UDALL, New Mexico	JOHN BARRASSO, Wyoming
CHRISTOPHER MURPHY, Connecticut	RAND PAUL, Kentucky
TIM KAINE, Virginia	

DANIEL E. O'BRIEN, *Staff Director*
LESTER E. MUNSON III, *Republican Staff Director*

(II)

CONTENTS

(III)

COUNTERTERRORISM POLICIES AND PRIORITIES: ADDRESSING THE EVOLVING THREAT

WEDNESDAY, MARCH 20, 2013

U.S. Senate,
Committee on Foreign Relations,
Washington, DC.

The committee met, pursuant to notice, at 4:35 p.m., in room SD–419, Dirksen Senate Office Building, Hon. Robert Menendez (chairman of the committee) presiding.

Present: Senators Menendez, Murphy, Kaine, and Corker.

OPENING STATEMENT OF HON. ROBERT MENENDEZ, U.S. SENATOR FROM NEW JERSEY

The Chairman. This hearing of the Senate Foreign Relations Committee will come to order.

Let me first apologize to our panel. There are some things beyond my control, like when we vote. Unfortunately, a series of votes were called for 2:15, which is when we would have been in the midst of the hearing, and I thought they were going to end by 4 o'clock, by my calculation; but, sometimes the best calculations in the world go challenged. We just had the last vote, on continuing to keep the government open. So, I appreciate your forbearance, your willingness to stay and enrich the committee with your knowledge. And you have our thanks and our gratitude for waiting.

Today, as we investigate counterterrorism policies and priorities to address the evolving threat we face, we want to thank our panelists for being here today.

We know the core of al-Qaeda has been significantly degraded. We know that Ayman al-Zawahiri is not Osama bin Laden, and that the central organization is, as many have stated, on a path of decline that will be difficult to reverse. But, the threat that remains is now decentralized. We still live in a challenging world. Al-Qaeda affiliates and other emerging extremist groups still pose a threat to the United States and our national interests.

Last week, this committee held a classified hearing, with Under Secretary Wendy Sherman and NCTC Director Matt Olsen, to gain a deeper understanding of the threats we face, the true extent of the links between and among extremist groups, and what that means for U.S. national interests.

From Al Qaeda in Iraq to Al Qaeda in the Islamic Maghreb, from al-Shabaab to Lashkar-e-Taiba, emerging extremist groups use al-Qaeda ties for financial assistance, training, arms, and mes- saging purposes. At the same time, they are often pursuing independent goals. Groups like Al Qaeda in the Arabian Peninsula have emerged as one of the most dangerous threats to the United States, targeting the U.S. Embassy in Yemen, and making at least three unsuccessful attempts to bomb airlines over United States airspace.

We also know that many of these extremist groups are internally divided, torn between a local agenda and more global set of goals. We need an effective strategy to counter these new threats without losing sight of al-Qaeda's beleaguered core in Pakistan.

Finally, the threat from extremist groups is not just a military and intelligence challenge, it is a foreign policy challenge, as well. We ask our diplomats to operate in often dangerous, high-threat areas made all the more unpredictable by these extremist groups. As we think through ways to better protect our diplomats, we must also consider ways to make our foreign policy more resilient to these ever-changing and irregular threats. We need to look at every tool in our toolkit, from development efforts to long-term governance-building initiatives. From Somalia to Mali, we have seen that weak governance only adds fuel to the proverbial fire. It gives extremist groups the space they need to train, recruit, and plan.

We also need to refine our efforts to understand and address root causes of extremism and better target the recruitment pipeline, and we need to strengthen and build our global partnerships. In my view, we need to take a step back and look at the whole board, and see the whole picture from every angle if we are to develop a comprehensive counterterrorism policy, and that is why we are here today.

The questions before us are clear. Yes, we have had tremendous success in decimating al-Qaeda, but the threats have shifted, and we need to know to what extent these new threats put us and our allies at risk. Given this new paradigm, do we need to revisit our approaches and reassess our overall strategy? How has the Arab Spring and other recent events changed both the threats and our options?

To answer these questions today, we are fortunate to have three highly knowledgeable witnesses: Congresswoman Jane Harman, the director, president, and CEO of the Woodrow Wilson Center for International Scholars, and a former nine-term Congresswoman from California who has served on the Armed Services, Intelligence, and Homeland Security Committees; Mike Leiter, who is currently the senior counselor to the chief executive of Palantir Technologies, and the former Director of the National Counterterrorism Center under Presidents Bush and Obama; and Ken Wainstein, currently a partner at Cadwalader, and formerly the Assistant to President Bush for Homeland Security and Counterterrorism.

Again, thanks to all of you.

Let me turn to the Ranking Member, Senator Corker.

OPENING STATEMENT OF HON. BOB CORKER, U.S. SENATOR FROM TENNESSEE

Senator CORKER. Thank you all. And our apologies for what has happened today. I think you know we had a CR that took a little longer than the norm, but we are glad you are here. And this will play a role as we shape things, going forward, even at 4:35 in the afternoon. So, thank you very much.

Today, the Foreign Relations Committee is convening its second counterterrorism hearing of the 113th Congress, and its first open hearing on these matters.

Given recent events around the world, and the growing influence of the al-Qaeda brand in places such as Syria and North and West Africa, I think the chairman's decision to hold these hearings is timely.

I recently traveled to North and West Africa, where I had a chance to meet with key foreign leaders, our State Department, and other U.S. Government personnel to discuss with them the evolving threat posed by al-Qaeda, both in Africa and around the world. What struck me most clearly, when considering groups like Al Qaeda in the Islamic Maghreb, is that the evolution of al-Qaeda really requires an evolution of our response and strategy.

First, the United States cannot do it all on its own. We must work with other countries around the world, not just Western countries, but the countries in which al-Qaeda operates, no matter how difficult. Poorly governed and ungoverned space presents an especially difficult challenge in this respect.

Second, the evolution of al-Qaeda from a core-based entity to one that has nodes around the world presents an entirely different challenge than what we understood to be the threat in the aftermath of 9/11. I hope this hearing will allow us to have a full and frank discussion about the evolving threat posed by al-Qaeda, and the U.S. Government's response to this threat.

In particular, I would like to discuss the need for Congress to play a more active role in authorizing the use of force, in this conflict as well as others, and the need for Congress to help set appropriate policies for confronting these threats. We must ask and answer whether the act of Congress, over a decade ago, that sought to address the threat of al-Qaeda meets the requirements of today.

We must also ask whether it is appropriate for Congress to play what has been largely a consultive role in the process of our prosecution of this war against al-Qaeda, and whether that meets our constitutional duties.

I hope this hearing is the beginning of an effort by this committee, which has an exclusive jurisdiction in authorizing the use of force, to look at these hard issues and to make the tough calls that we were elected to make on behalf of the American people.

And I thank you and look forward to your testimony today.

The CHAIRMAN. Thank you, Senator Corker.

With that, let me invite Congresswoman Harman to start off.

Your full statements will be entered into the record, and we will look forward to having a conversation with you once you are finished.

STATEMENT OF HON. JANE HARMAN, DIRECTOR, PRESIDENT, AND CEO, WOODROW WILSON INTERNATIONAL CENTER FOR SCHOLARS, FORMER MEMBER, U.S. HOUSE OF REPRESENTATIVES, WASHINGTON, DC

Ms. HARMAN. Thank you, Mr. Chairman and Ranking Member Corker. I served with both of you during my long time on the Hill,

4

and I commend you both for staying in the game. And I hope you voted to keep the Government open. Did you?

The CHAIRMAN. Yes.

Ms. HARMAN. That is a relief. Then it was worth waiting.

The CHAIRMAN. That is a bipartisan "yes," so——

Ms. HARMAN. As the former Member of Congress, here, I will defer to my good friends for more of the tactical discussion, but I thought I would raise a bigger policy issue, at least it is one that troubles me, because I think that the Foreign Relations Committee needs to consider this, beyond just the assertion of kinetic power, to defeat—and we have defeated—some of these enemies. And as I reflect on my own role, and the role of many who tried to keep us safe after 9/11, I think we got the tactics right, but my point today is, we got the strategy wrong. We have yet to develop a narrative, a positive-sum roadmap for where we are going and why others will benefit by joining us.

Stan McChrystal recently was interviewed by Foreign Affairs magazine, and he nailed it, at least the way I think about it. He said that, when he first was involved with Iraq and Afghanistan, he asked, "Where's the enemy?" As things evolved, he then asked, "Who is the enemy?" Then he asked, "What is the enemy trying to do?" And finally, the question that he asked was, "Why is he the enemy?" And that is something that is sobering and I really think we have to think about.

I am betting you agree with me that we cannot kill our way to victory, because kinetics alone are more likely to inflame than persuade. But, what is the United States doing to persuade? Are we coordinated? Are we delivering the same message? I want to say our tactics have had an impact. And, as you said, Mr. Chairman, we have certainly decimated core al-Qaeda. But, now al-Qaeda has morphed into a more horizontal organization, and the question is, Is that growing? And are some of the things we are doing causing it to grow?

I think I will skip how the threat has changed, because you will hear it from my friends, but just to point out that the 10th issue of Inspire magazine is back online and as savvy as ever. Extremist digital natives have also created something called Muslim Mali. It is a computer game that simulates aerial combat against French fighter jets and is designed to inspire fellow extremists to take up arms against the French. Once a user clicks "Play," an Arabic message appears with the words, "Muslim brother, go ahead and repel the French invasion against Muslim Mali." And this kind of propaganda is appearing in many places. And to beat this propaganda, we really have to win the argument with some kid in the rural parts of Yemen deciding whether to strap on a suicide vest or join society. And what I am saying is, we may not be winning that argument.

So, quickly, let me just go to some recommendations.

First, stop piecemeal counterterrorism policy and implementation. Stop stovepiped one-off CT efforts and create a whole-of-government strategy. Give the Department of State's CT Bureau more support to do its job. This is within your jurisdiction. The Antiterrorism Assistance Program, Countering Violent Extremism Grants, and coordinating efforts through the Center for Strategic

Counterterrorism Communications, all a mouthful, are important, but not adequate. A more robust CT Bureau could help us better find the gaps in our nonkinetic efforts, and to fill those gaps.

Two, smarter investments. Carefully analyze foreign aid budgets and find ways to plus-up funds to countries that need it most, and resist funding flavor-of-the-month countries.

Third, live our values. Our actions really do speak louder than words. Semantics like "rendition," "enhanced interrogation," "targeted killing" fuel the terror propaganda machine. We have a perception problem and have to apply a matrix of our interests and our values, and test it against our future engagements. Again, we have got to win the argument, not just play "Whac-a-Mole." We need a public conversation about tactics and strategy, and that is what this hearing is designed to do, and I commend you for holding it.

Fourth, reduce overclassification of intelligence. Far too much information is classified. Instead of safeguarding our secrets, we are actually preventing ourselves from seeing the bigger threat picture. One of my last accomplishments in Congress was to author something called the Reducing Overclassification Act, which President Obama signed in October 2010. I do not really know that it has led to much. I still think this problem needs attention.

Finally, we have to drain the swamp. And, as a scholar at the Wilson Center, Aaron David Miller, suggests, we will reduce the pool of potential terrorists by encouraging reform efforts by authoritarian governments. Secretary Kerry understands this, and hopefully will implement it.

In conclusion, I urge you to play a major role in developing this overdue strategy. After all, it is foreign relationships, not more foreign enemies, that we need.

Thank you.

[The prepared statement of Ms. Harman follows:]

PREPARED STATEMENT OF HON. JANE HARMAN

TACTICS V. STRATEGY

It is fitting that this committee—the Foreign Relations Committee—is holding this hearing. As I reflect on my own role and the role of many who tried just as hard to keep us safe after 9/11, we got many of the tactics right but the strategy wrong. We have yet to develop a narrative, a positive-sum roadmap for where we are going and why others will benefit by joining with us.

Retired General Stanley McChrystal—former head of Special Operations Command and the International Security Assistance Force in Afghanistan—recently nailed it. In an interview in Foreign Affairs on Iraq and Afghanistan, he first asked "Where is the enemy?" As the engagement evolved, he asked "Who is the enemy?" Then, "What is the enemy trying to do?" Finally, he realized the question we most needed to answer was: "Why is he the enemy?"

This realization is bone-chilling. Many senior policymakers know we cannot kill our way to victory—because kinetics alone are more likely to inflame than persuade. But what is the United States doing to persuade? Are we coordinated in our actions? Are we delivering the same message?

Our tactics have an impact—and playing whack-a-mole will not win the argument with the kid in rural Syria or Yemen deciding whether or not to strap on a suicide vest.

EVOLUTION OF THE THREAT

How has the threat evolved over time? We all know that what once was a highly centralized structure—Core Al Qaeda leadership—has been decimated. But, rather than disappear, it has morphed into a decentralized horizontal organization—composed mainly of so-called ''affiliates.''

Our adversaries—many of them young, digital natives—have spent the past few years—while the United States focused on eliminating core leadership—building up their propaganda elements and their recruiting shop. Smaller scale, easier to accomplish attacks are now the name of the game—in an effort to cause as much chaos as possible.

Inspire magazine is back online and as savvy as ever. Extremist digital natives have created a ''Muslim Mali'' computer game that simulates aerial combat against French fighter jets, and is designed to inspire fellow extremists to take up arms against the French. Once a user clicks ''play,'' an Arabic message appears with the words, ''Muslim Brother, go ahead and repel the French invasion against Muslim Mali.''

These digital natives can sit in their homes or computer cafes anywhere in the world. What really keeps me up at night? That this generation will turn to cyber attacks—even small ones, because the information is sitting right at their fingertips. Let me be clear: the United States is not just facing Chinese hackers seeking ballistic missile blueprints or Russian hackers trying to steal credit card numbers. We also face nonstate actors who have drunk the al-Qaeda Kool-Aid.

THE NEXT TEN YEARS

Despite astonishing adaptation since 9/11—including a massive reform of the intelligence community, in which I played a fairly big role—Uncle Sam is still built for yesterday's threats.

So, what do we do?

Christopher Paul of the RAND Corporation says: ''The trick . . . is to apprehend or otherwise deal with [the] residual threat without creating a chain of events that renews motivations for participation and support.''

Here are my recommendations:

1. Stop piecemeal counterterrorism policy and implementation

- Stop stovepiped, one-off CT efforts and create a whole-of-government strategy. Excuses about bureaucratic inertia and the number of people involved should not stop us from doing what is necessary. This includes our cyber defenses.
- Give the Department of State's CT Bureau more support to do its job. The Antiterrorism Assistance Program, Countering Violent Extremism grants, and coordinating efforts through the Center for Strategic Counterterrorism Communications are all important but just not enough. A more robust CT Bureau could help us better find gaps in our nonkinetic efforts and fill them.

2. Smarter investments

Carefully analyze the foreign aid budgets and find ways to plus-up funds to the countries that need it most—and resist funding for the flavor-of-the-month countries. Foreign aid is in many cases the only leverage we have—and should have serious strings attached. This will also be a very difficult task—and requires a clear, reasoned message to the American people about why such targeted investments are necessary for the U.S. Secretary of State, John Kerry, has urged similar efforts as has a senior Republican Senator.

3. Live our values

- Our actions really do speak louder than words. It should be no wonder that the semantics America used in the past—when extra judicial kidnapping became ''rendition,'' torture became ''enhanced interrogation,'' and assassination became ''targeted killing''—only fueled the terror propaganda machine. We have a perception problem.
- We must apply a matrix of our interests and our values, and test against it our future engagements. Then we stand a better chance at defeating the negative narrative being created about us. That means paying more than lip service to privacy protections, and considering legal protections, especially regarding ''Big Data.'' Trying more terror suspects in U.S. Federal courts—like Sulaiman Abu Ghaith—is also the right move.
- We need a public conversation about tactics and strategy, and Congress should legislate clear limits. Self-policing by the executive branch was wrong in the Bush 43 administration, and is wrong now. I have recently suggested that FISA could be adapted to cover drones and offensive cyber.

4. Reduce overclassification of intelligence

- Far too much information is classified. Instead of safeguarding our secrets, we are actually preventing ourselves from seeing the bigger threat picture. If we can't see all the ''dots'' of intelligence, how could we hope to get ahead of future threats?

5. Drain the swamp

- As Wilson Center Scholar Aaron David Miller suggests, we will reduce the pool of potential terrorists by encouraging reform efforts by authoritarian governments. Secretary Kerry's efforts to persuade the Egyptians to move forward with reforms are an example of what we need more of.

CONCLUSION

In conclusion, I urge this committee to play a major role in developing this overdue strategy. After all, it is foreign relationships—not more foreign enemies—that we need.

The CHAIRMAN. Thank you very much.
Mr. Leiter.

STATEMENT OF HON. MICHAEL E. LEITER, SENIOR COUNSELOR TO THE CHIEF EXECUTIVE OFFICER, PALANTIR TECHNOLOGIES, FORMER DIRECTOR OF THE NATIONAL COUNTERTERRORISM CENTER, McLEAN, VA

Mr. LEITER. Mr. Chairman, Ranking Member Corker, members of the committee, thanks for having me.

I would note that, in my 4 years at the National Counterterrorism Center, I do not believe I ever testified before the Senate Foreign Relations Committee, which, I have to tell you, is not a good sign, and I think it is a good sign that you are holding these hearings today and the Director of NCTC is here before you, because this is not just an intel, not just an Armed Services issue, this is very much for the Senate Foreign Relations Committee. So, I am very happy you are doing it.

In my written testimony, I go through, in some detail, my assessment of the threat. I am not going to rehash that here, but I do want to highlight a few things.

First of all, in my view, we are in a better position to detect and disrupt a catastrophic attack like we saw on 9/11 than anytime since 2001. We have done very, very well in this fight.

That being said, as both of you have already noted, we do face a fragmented threat, but I would urge this committee not to read too much into some of the recent events. They are undoubtedly tragic; I do not mean to minimize the attack in Benghazi and the death of four Americans, the attack in Algeria, the rise of AQIM. But, in terms of large-scale, catastrophic threats to the homeland, these are not anywhere remotely on the same page. They threaten U.S. interests. We will always, have always, and will continue to face threats in these regions. We must continue to battle the terrorists, as Jane Harman said, drain the swamp, all these things; but, on average, I think we should actually be enormously proud of the Congress, the executive branch, and, to some extent, the courts, in enabling a fight against terrorism that has been pretty successful.

Now, I do want to highlight a couple of areas where I think we do face enormous challenges. We have mentioned North Africa already. I think the other key place that we have to really recognize a huge threat to the United States is Syria and what we see in the al-Nusra Front. We are seeing a magnet for foreign fighters, and we see enormous instability and tension between Shias and Sunnis, with access to weapons of mass destruction. And this is, if not an existential threat, certainly an existential threat to our interests in the region.

Second, one that is, unfortunately, often forgotten in these hearings, Hezbollah. And especially as tensions increase between the United States, Iran, and Israel, and what was going on in Syria, we have to keep our eye on Hezbollah, who has gotten increasingly aggressive, both with kinetic strikes—the attack in Bulgaria, killing Israeli tourists—and also, destructive cyber attacks against Saudi Aramco and RasGas in Qatar. Both of these are signs that Hezbollah is, indeed, moving toward a more aggressive approach; the United States and our allies.

Now, with that, let me offer four quick observations on things that I think this committee should, in fact, focus on; vis-a-vis, terrorism, writ large.

First, after 10-plus years, we really do, I believe, face a terrorism fatigue problem. And that is, we have been talking about this for 10 years, and people want to move on. And that poses a real challenge, because we need to have discussions to make sure that our tools to combat terrorism are on a solid footing. In that regard, I am extremely heartened about the conversations we have seen in the public and with Congress over the past several months about targeted killings and potentially reforming the authorization for use of military force. I believe these are exactly the conversations we need to have so these do have a strong footing for the years to come.

Second, for terrorism fatigue, I am extremely worried that, with every terrorist attack, we now view it as a systemic failure rather than, to some extent, a fact of life in counterterrorism work. And I am all for examining these events after the fact to see how we can do better, but I would plead with this committee that these do not become ex-post investigations and excoriations of terrorism professionals, because it will chase the good people out of government.

Last, I do think that terrorism fatigue affects the executive branch, and I am very worried that things that the executive branch needs to push on quickly and hard, like information-sharing, fall by the wayside.

Second significant issue: weapons of mass destruction. We are, I think, faced with small-scale attacks, no matter what we do. These are tragic, but we will live with them, and we will prosper. Weapons with mass destruction pose a very different threat. And securing nuclear material, trying to prevent improvised nuclear devices, trying to prevent complex biological weapons attacks, they are low-probability, but enormous-consequence events, and we must keep our eye on these things. And this committee has a huge role in that way.

Third, counterterrorism partnerships. With terrorism fatigue has become a fatiguing of the partnerships that we rely on. And, as you said, Senator Corker, especially in regions of Middle East and North Africa, these partnerships, both in willingness and capacity, have frayed significantly, and we have to work very hard to work closely with our partners to maintain them and maintain the programs within the U.S. Government to support those partners.

And, last but not least, staying on the offense on all fronts. And, to me, that means continuing programs of targeting killing, where we have to take people off the battlefield, but, equally if not more importantly, expanding our efforts on soft power, because kinetic focus has, in fact, sapped much of the focus within the executive branch of putting the resources and the time and energy into those things that take time to, as Jane said, drain the swamp and reduce the attraction of terrorism.

And last, covering all of these things, as you all know from having just voted on continuing to open the government, after 12 years we have poured—it is difficult to estimate, but probably about $100 billion each year into counterterrorism efforts, including Iraq and Afghanistan. This money is not going to be there in the future. So, this is exactly the time that we have to do a far more rational look at mission-focused budgeting—not department by department, but mission—to understand where we can put our limited dollars that we have to get the biggest bang for the buck for the whole of the U.S. Government.

Thank you.

[The prepared statement of Mr. Leiter follows:]

PREPARED STATEMENT OF HON. MICHAEL E. LEITER

OVERVIEW

Chairman Menendez, Ranking Member Corker, and members of the committee, thank you for inviting me to testify on my perspectives on the evolving threat of terrorism and how it can be best addressed by the United States and our allies. I believe now is an opportune time to take stock of the threat we face and our associated response. While we have made remarkable strides against the threat of catastrophic attacks like that which we experienced on 9/11, the continued presence of al-Qaeda in Yemen, the growing presence of al-Qaeda-associated elements in North Africa and Syria, and increased instability across North Africa and the Middle East highlight how the threat of terrorism continues. Combined with a fiscal reality that precludes the sort of spending we have maintained since 2001, this is a historic moment to rationalize and calibrate our response to terrorism and related threats to our national security.

THE THREAT LANDSCAPE

Today al-Qaeda and its allies in Pakistan are at their weakest point since 9/11. The death of Osama bin Laden and the continued decimation of senior ranks has made the organization a shadow of its former self. Ayman al-Zawahiri is not bin Laden and although the organization still attempts to provide strategic guidance and global propaganda, its influence continues to wane. Whether this trajectory can be maintained with a significant decrease of the U.S. presence in Afghanistan and a continued challenging political landscape in Pakistan will be, in my view, the biggest determinants of al-Qaeda Core's relevance for the coming decade.

The degradation of al-Qaeda's ''higher headquarters'' and relatively well-coordinated command and control has allowed its affiliates and its message to splinter, posing new dangers and challenges. Al Qa'ida affiliates or those inspired by its message have worrisome presences in Yemen, East Africa, North Africa, Syria, Western Europe, and of course to a lesser degree the United States.

Beginning with Yemen, in my view Al Qaeda in the Arabian Peninsula (AQAP)— as I stated 2 years ago—continues to pose the most sophisticated and deadly threat to the U.S. homeland from an overseas affiliate. The death of operational commander Anwar al-Aulaqi significantly reduced AQAP's ability to attract and motivate English speakers, but its operational efforts continue with lesser abatement. As we saw in 2009, 2010, and 2012, AQAP has remained committed—and able— to pursue complex attacks involving innovative improvised explosives devices. Although some of the organization's safe haven has been diminished because of

Yemeni and U.S. efforts, the inability of the Government of Yemen to bring true control to wide swaths of the country suggests that the group will pose a threat for the foreseeable future and (unlike many other affiliates) it clearly remains focused on transnational attacks.

East Africa, surprisingly to many, is a brighter spot in our efforts. Although al-Shabaab remains a force and poses significant risks in the region—most especially in Kenya and to the fledgling government in Somalia—its risk to the homeland is markedly less today than just 2 years ago. Kenya's offensive in the region shattered much of al-Shabaab's power base and most importantly the attractiveness of Somalia to Americans and other Westerners is radically less than was the case. The relative flood of Americans has turned into a trickle, thus significantly reducing the threat of trained terrorists returning to our shores. Maintaining this positive momentum will require continued U.S. attention and close cooperation with the African Union in Somalia (AMISOM) to nurture what clearly remains a fragile recovery.

As the world witnessed over the past 6 months, Al Qaeda in the Islamic Maghreb (AQIM) has shifted the focus in Africa as the organization has made gains in Mali, Libya, and the rural areas of Algeria. To be clear, to those of us in the counter-terrorism ranks this is not particularly surprising. In my view while the attacks in Benghazi and on the Algerian oil facility are tragic, the major change to the region is not a massive increase in AQIM's attractiveness, but rather the huge shift that occurred with the virtual elimination of Libya's security services, the associated flood of weapons in the region, and the coup d'etat in Mali.

AQIM has thus far proven a less tactically proficient and more regionally focused criminal organization than other al-Qaeda affiliates. Although we cannot blindly hope this remains the case, I would argue that we should also not read too much into recent events. Regional capacity building, targeted offensive measures, and forceful engagement with government like France, Algeria, and Libya that have a huge vested interest in the region should remain at the forefront of our strategy. And we must roundly condemn (and try to limit) the payment of ransoms that have proven to be the lifeblood of AQIM and its affiliates.

One notable area of concern that we must forcefully combat in the region—and one which the United States is uniquely able to address given our global footprint—is the cross-fertilization across the African Continent that has recently accelerated. Coordination amongst al-Shabaab, AQIM, Boko Haram, and others is particularly problematic as it allows each organization to leverage the others' strengths. We must use our intelligence capabilities to define these networks and then assist in disrupting them.

The most troubling of emerging fronts in my view is Syria, where Jabhat al-Nusra has emerged as the most radical of groups within the opposition. Given the enormous instability in Syria, which has to some degree already spread to Iraq and elsewhere in the Levant, Jabhat al-Nusra has become a magnet for al-Qaeda-inspired fighters from around the globe. With virtually no likelihood of rapid improvements in Syria (and a not insignificant risk of rapid decline caused by the use of chemical or biological weapons), the al-Nusra front will almost certainly continue to arm, obtain real world combat experience, and attract additional recruits—and potentially state assistance that is flowing to the FSA.

Moreover, Jabhat al-Nusra's ideology not only contributes to the threat of terrorism, but more broadly it is contributing significantly to the regional Sunni-Shia tension that poses enormous risks. The rapid removal of Bashar al-Assad would not solve these problems, but an ongoing civil war does in my view worsen the situation. Although there is no easy answer to this devilish issue, I believe that with the U.K.'s recent movement to providing lethal assistance to the FSA, we too should move more forcefully with additional aid and the creating of safe havens in border areas.

Without declaring victory, we should also have some optimism about al-Qaeda-inspired terrorism in Western Europe and especially the homeland. As recent studies have shown, there has been a continuing decline in numbers of significant homeland plots that have not been closely controlled by the FBI since 2009. In addition, the relative sophistication of homeland terrorists has not increased. Combined with successful counterterrorism efforts in Western Europe—most particularly huge strides in the U.K.—the picture faced today is far brighter than just 3 years ago.

Similar optimism cannot be applied to the threat posed by Lebanese Hezbollah, especially given its successful and foiled attacks over the past 2 years. Most notably, Hezbollah attack in Bulgaria killed six tourists and highlights the extent to which the group (and its patrons in Iran) continue to see themselves as being in an ongoing unconventional war with Israel and the United States. Predicting Hezbollah and Iranian ''redlines'' is a notoriously challenging endeavor—as illustrated by the surprising 2011 plot to kill the Saudi Ambassador to the U.S.—but both organizations almost certainly would launch attacks at least outside the U.S. were there a strike on Iranian nuclear facilities.

There is little doubt that both Hezbollah and the IRGC Qods Force maintain a network of operatives that could be used for such strikes. In this regard the heavy Iranian presence in Latin America and Iranian cooperation with former Venezuelan President Hugo Chavez is of particular concern. Although not every Hezbollah member and Iranian diplomat is a trained operative, a significant number could in the case of hostilities enable other operatives to launch attacks against Israeli or U.S. diplomatic facilities, Jewish cultural institutions, or high profile individuals.

In addition, and generally unlike al-Qaeda affiliates, the specter of Hezbollah or Iranian-sponsored cyber attacks is disturbingly real. Recent Distributed Denial of Service (DDOS) attacks on major U.S. financial institutions, as well as even more destructive Iranian-sponsored attacks on Saudi Aramco and Qatar-based RasGas, have highlighted the extent to which physical attacks might be combined with cyber attacks.

LOOKING AHEAD

This threat picture, although complex and dynamic, is in many ways more heartening than that which we faced from 2001 until at least 2010. Numerous organizations continue to threaten terrorist attacks, but as a very general matter the threats are away from the homeland and the scale of the attacks is markedly less than what we saw in September 2001 or even 2006, when al-Qaeda came dangerously close to attacking up to 10 transatlantic airliners. It is not that events like Benghazi are not tragic. But threats to U.S. diplomatic facilities in Libya are of a radically different type than planes flying into civilian facilities in New York and Washington. In this regard, this is an appropriate juncture to look at a few of our biggest risks and challenges.

Terrorism Fatigue. After 10-plus years of near constant public discussion of terrorism—in our politics, the media, and through public messaging—many have simply had enough. This is not all bad as an unhealthy obsession with the threat of terrorism at the expense of countless other societal woes, such as cyber threats and Iranian nuclear ambitions, would in many ways hand our enemy a victory. On the other hand, there is real value in public discussion of terrorism: it can build resilience in the population and it can lead to the tackling of tough public policy questions like targeted killings and domestic intelligence. With terrorism fatigue we run a real risk of not addressing these issues in a way that provides a lasting counterterrorism framework. In this regard I actually see the current discussion around the use of drones and the potential for updating the 2001 Authorization for the Use of Military Force as quite heartening signs.

Terrorism fatigue poses at least two additional challenges. First, with all of our counterterrorism success such victories have become expected and any failure—no matter how small—can result in political finger pointing and excoriation of our counterterrorism professionals. In effect we have become victims of our own success and unlike in 2001, perfection has become a political expectation. Although we should continuously examine how we can improve our capabilities, we must guard against ex poste investigations that lack a serious appreciation for the ex ante difficulties of counterterrorism.

Second, terrorism fatigue can cause dangerous lethargy within the executive branch on issues that do not appear to require immediate attention but which can do longer term damage to counterterrorism efforts. I have repeatedly seen urgency morph into bureaucratic sluggishness as time passes since the last attack on issues like information-sharing and interagency cooperation. Whether it is countering violent extremism programs or information access for the intelligence community, we must not take our foot off the gas pedal.

Weapons of Mass Destruction. There is no doubt that smallish terrorist attacks or at least attempts will continue to occur at home and abroad. Such attacks can cause enormous pain and suffering to victims and their families, but they are clearly of a scale—at least with respect to absolute numbers killed—that is dwarfed by other societal ills such as routine criminal activity. The same cannot be said of terrorists' use of weapons of mass destruction—and more specifically biological weapons or an improvised nuclear device (IND).

Although we have also made progress in reducing the likelihood of terrorists obtaining WMD, for the foreseeable future we are faced with the possibility that a terrorist organization will successfully acquire these weapons. In this case, technology is not yet our friend as the ease with which these weapons can be obtained and hidden continues to exceed our ability to detect them.

Weapons of mass destruction pose a unique challenge as they are the prototypical low likelihood, high consequence event and thus determining the proper allocation of resources to combat them is particular contentious. That being said, we must continue to protect against the most dangerous of materials (e.g., HEU) being obtained by terrorists, secure weapons in the most dangerous places (e.g., Pakistan and increasingly Syria), and pursue research and development that will assist in detecting chemical and biological weapons in places where they would do the most harm.

Counterterrorism Partnerships. Counterterrorism has always been and continues to be a "team sport." Although the United States can do much alone, we have always been incredibly reliant on a vast network of friendly nations that have extended massively our intelligence, law enforcement, military, and homeland security reach. Even before the Arab Awakening we witnessed some weakening of these partnerships. Whether it was fatigue on our partners' part, their own resource challenges, or differing views on the proper scope of counterterrorist efforts (e.g., fights over data sharing between the United States and the European Union), these partnerships have been under some pressure. Post-Arab Awakening we face an exponentially more daunting task, having lost some of our most valuable partners—and key security services even where political leadership remains supportive—in the very places we need them most.

Again, part of the challenge is that we have been a victim of our own success. Al-Qaeda is simply not viewed as the same existential threat that it was in 2001. But without robust partnerships it will be increasingly difficult for us to detect and disrupt rising al-Qaeda (or other groups') cells, thus making it more likely that they will metastasize and embed themselves in ways that makes them more dangerous and more difficult to displace.

To maintain our partnerships we must carefully preserve funding for programs that provide critical capabilities—and potentially more important, a positive U.S. presence—for our allies. The increase in funding for special operations forces is a good step, but relatively tiny investments in Department of State and Justice programs can also deliver real results in this realm. In addition, we will have to approach new governments in the Middle East with sophistication and ensure they continue to view terrorism as a mutual threat.

Staying on the Offense—on all Fronts. Over the past month an enormous amount has been said about targeted killings, especially of U.S. persons. In my view, having served under both Presidents George W. Bush and Obama, such targeted killings are a vital tool in the counterterrorism toolbox. And regrettably, in some cases that tool must also be used against U.S. persons like Anwar al-Aulaqi who was a senior al-Qaeda operational commander who was continuing to plot attacks against the United States.

From my perspective, the memorandum and administration practice (contrary to claims by some) appropriately constrains the President's authority, has provided significant congressional oversight and the opportunity to limit the program, and provides realistic standards given the inherent challenges of intelligence and counterterrorism.

As I have previously implied, however, I am equally supportive of the current public debate on the issue. In fact, I believe bringing greater visibility to some programs could be useful not only to build U.S. support, but also to build greater international understanding if not support—a key element in our ideological efforts. Moreover, I would suggest that the current debate highlights the need to examine seriously the 2001 Authorization for the Use of Military Force (AUMF). During my tenure at the National Counterterrorism Center the AUMF provided adequate authority for the use of force, but it was not always a simple or straightforward application. With the continued evolution of the terror threat and most notably its increasing distance from the 9/11 attacks and Core Al Qaeda, I believe it is the time to reevaluate the AUMF to better fit today's threat landscape.

As supportive as I am of targeted killings in appropriate circumstances, I am equally (if not more) supportive of ensuring that these are not our only counterterrorism tools employed. I do believe that our reliance on kinetic strikes has in some cases allowed other efforts to atrophy or at least pale in comparison. This is enormously dangerous, as we cannot strike everywhere nor can we lethally target an ideology. As we increase targeted killings we must double down on our soft power and ideological efforts—building capacity in civilian security forces, increasing the rule of law to diminish undergoverned or ungoverned safe havens, and the like—lest we win a few battles and lose a global war. This committee must stand at the very center of these efforts, as I fear in the current fiscal climate that the programs that support our ideological efforts will be given short shrift.

Resources. Finally, and not entirely inappropriately, counterterrorism resources will undoubtedly decline significantly in the coming years. It is difficult to estimate accurately how much has been spent on counterterrorism over the past 11 years, but the amount certainly comes close if not exceeds $100 billion a year. Some of this was undoubtedly well spent, but it is folly to think that inefficiencies and redundancies do not exist widely. In this sense, a bit of frugality is likely a very good thing.

The question, however, is whether we will be willing or able to make smart reductions to preserve critical capabilities. Our historic ability to direct funds where the threat is greatest—as opposed to where the political forces are strongest—have not been good. Perhaps the declining threat will mean that we can continue to spend imperfectly, but this is surely a dangerous bet to make.

We should use this imposed frugality to do serious mission-based—as opposed to Department and Agency-specific based—budgeting in the Federal Government. This approach will require enormous changes within the executive and congressional branches, but looking across the counterterrorism budget, identifying the critical capabilities we must preserve, and then figuring out how that matches Department-specific budgets can be done. And if we are serious about maintaining these capabilities we have little choice.

CONCLUSION

More than a decade after 9/11, combating terrorism isn't over. No one should be surprised by this fact. Nor should anyone be surprised that we are fighting in different places and, although some approaches are the same as they were in 2001, many of our tools must evolve with the evolving threat. Moreover, having the benefit of almost 12 years of national effort we are in a better place today to balance our counterterrorism efforts with other significant threats to our national security, most notably state-sponsored cyber intrusions, theft, and attacks, and broad instability across much of North Africa and the Middle East.

Thank you for inviting me to testify, and for this committee's leadership on these critical issues. I look forward to working with this committee to ensure that we as a nation are protecting our citizens, our allies, and our interests from the scourge of terrorism.

The CHAIRMAN. Thank you very much.
Mr. Wainstein.

STATEMENT OF HON. KENNETH L. WAINSTEIN, PARTNER, CADWALADER, WICKERSHAM & TAFT, LLP, FORMER ASSISTANT TO THE PRESIDENT FOR HOMELAND SECURITY AND COUNTERTERRORISM, WASHINGTON, DC

Mr. WAINSTEIN. Chairman Menendez, Ranking Member Corker, Senator Kaine, I want to thank the three of you and the committee for the invitation to join in this discussion of the evolving threat that our Nation faces today.

And it is a particular pleasure for me to be here with my two copanelists and colleagues, who are proven experts in this field and have devoted much of their professional lives to protecting our country against terrorist adversaries.

It is vitally important that we, as a nation, continually gauge our readiness to meet the evolving threat that we face. And we have seen the consequences of failing to do that throughout our recent history. Go back to 1941, when we were completely unready for the threat that struck us at Pearl Harbor. We built up after that and ultimately defeated the Axis Powers, and then the subsequent Soviet threat of the cold war, but then we sort of dropped our guard again a little bit when we failed to anticipate the looming threat that was posed by globally connected terrorist organizations like al-Qaeda.

Since 9/11, the last two administrations have made tremendous efforts to bring our counterterrorism readiness back in line with the post-9/11 threat. As a result of these efforts, as Mike Leiter just said, we, as a nation, are significantly better prepared to meet that threat than we were on the morning of 9/11, and I think there is no better gauge of that than—or evidence of that than—the number of top-echelon al-Qaeda leaders who are no longer on the battlefield and the list of terrorist plots that have been foiled over the past few years.

It has become clear, however, that the al-Qaeda threat that has occupied our attention and our focus since 9/11 is no longer the threat that we will need to defend against in the future. Due largely to the effectiveness of our counterterrorism operations, the centralized leadership of al-Qaeda that directed operations from the sanctuary that it held in Afghanistan and Pakistan, known as al-Qaeda core, is now just a shadow of what it once was. The result of that has been a migration of operational control and operational authority away from core al-Qaeda into al-Qaeda's affiliates in other regions of the world—Al Qaeda in the Arabian Peninsula, Al Qaeda in Iraq, and Al Qaeda in the Islamic Maghreb, to name a few.

In light of this evolution, we are now at a pivot point where we need to reevaluate the means and reevaluate the objectives of our counterterrorism program. And the executive branch, by all reports, is currently engaged in that process, and has made a number of policy shifts to reflect the altered threat landscape, including, for example, focusing on the development of stronger cooperative relationships with those countries, or governments in those countries, like Yemen, where these franchises are operating.

It is important, however, that Congress also participate closely in that process. Over the past 12 years, Congress has proven its value in the creation of the post-9/11 counterterrorism program. It has been instrumental in strengthening our counterterrorism capabilities. It has helped to create a lasting framework and structure for the long war against international terrorism. And its actions have provided one other very important element to our counterterrorism program, and that is a measure of political legitimacy that can never be achieved through unilateral executive action, alone. Therefore, as Mike Leiter just said, it is heartening to see that Congress is again starting to ratchet up its engagement in this area, with a discussion of a variety of different legislative proposals.

Now, in assessing these proposals, Congress should be guided by a pair of principles that it has largely followed over the past 12 years. First, it is important that any legal authorities that it consider be crafted in a way that permit operators and decisionmakers in the executive branch to act and react without undue delay. For instance, any scheme for regulating the use of targeted drone strikes should be designed with an appreciation for the need for quick decisionmaking and action in the context of war and targeting.

Second, Congress should continue to resist any legislation that unduly restricts the government's flexibility in the fight against international terrorists. Flexibility is the key to operational success in counterterrorism operations, and it should be the watchword for any national security legislation.

Congress is to be commended for having largely followed these principles over the last 12 years, and also commended for playing a vitally important role in the construction of our national counterterrorism program since 9/11, which is a role that Congress should continue to play in the years to come. And, as my colleague said, this committee is, specifically, to be commended for recognizing the recent evolution of the terrorist threat we are facing, and recognizing the need to reassess our strategy and our terrorism program in light of that evolution.

It has been an honor to be a part of that effort today, and I look forward to any questions that the committee may have.

[The prepared statement of Mr. Wainstein follows:]

PREPARED STATEMENT OF KENNETH L. WAINSTEIN

Chairman Menendez, Ranking Member Corker and members of the committee, thank you for the invitation to join in this discussion of the evolving threat that our Nation faces today. My name is Ken Wainstein, and I'm a partner at the law firm of Cadwalader, Wickersham & Taft. It is an honor to appear before you along with my two copanelists, both proven experts in this field who have devoted much of their professional lives to defending our Nation against its terrorist adversaries.

Today's topic is particularly timely, given that we are now seeing a transition in the scope and nature of the terrorist threat we face—a transition that requires us to assess whether we have the right counterterrorism strategy, organization, and authorities to successfully meet this evolving threat.

It is vitally important that we, as a nation, continually gauge our readiness to meet the threat we face. Our Nation's history since World War II illustrates both the importance and the mixed record of calibrating our readiness to meet overseas threats. In 1941, we found ourselves completely unready to meet the threat that struck us at Pearl Harbor. After building the warmaking machine that defeated the Axis Powers, we then recognized the new threat from the Soviet bloc and designed a governmental infrastructure and a foreign policy that successfully contained the Communist threat.

In the aftermath of the cold war, however, we let our guard down again. We enjoyed the peace dividend while the threat of international terrorism evolved from the relatively isolated operations of the Red Brigades, the Baader-Meinhof gang and the other violent groups of the 1970s into the more globally integrated organizations of the 1990s—a threat that emerged in its most virulent form in the network of violent extremists operating out of its safe haven under Taliban rule in Afghanistan.

Despite its potency, we did not reorient our defenses to meet this threat and continued to operate with an intelligence and military apparatus largely designed for the cold war. As we had in the 1930s when the storm of fascism was gathering overseas, we failed throughout the 1980s and 1990s to anticipate and prepare for the looming new threat posed by a globally networked terrorist organization with the resources, the operational sophistication and the fanatical following to mount a sustained campaign against the United States and its allies.

Since 9/11, the last two administrations have made tremendous efforts to bring our counterterrorism readiness more in line with the post-9/11 threat. These efforts have included a fundamental restructuring of our government's counterterrorism infrastructure, new and expanded investigative authorities for our intelligence and law enforcement personnel, the reorientation of our military to fight an asymmetric war against a nontraditional and shadowy foe, and the adoption of a foreign policy designed to enlist and coordinate with foreign partners in the global fight against international terrorism.

Thanks to the concerted efforts of both administrations, the past seven Congresses and countless committed public servants, we as a nation are significantly better prepared to meet the international terrorist threat than we were on the morning of 9/11. There is no better evidence of that fact than the number of top-echelon al-Qaeda leaders who have been removed from the battlefield and the list of terror- ist threats that have been foiled over the past few years.

It has recently become clear, however, that the al-Qaeda threat that occupied our attention after 9/11 is no longer the threat that we will need to defend against in the future. Due largely to the effectiveness of our counterterrorism efforts, the centralized leadership that had directed al-Qaeda operations from its sanctuary in Afghanistan and Pakistan—known as "Al Qaeda Core"—is now just a shadow of what it once was. While still somewhat relevant as an inspirational force, Zawahiri and his surviving lieutenants are reeling from our aerial strikes and no longer have the operational stability to manage an effective global terrorism campaign. The result has been a migration of operational authority and control from Al Qaeda Core to its affiliates in other regions of the world, such as Al Qaeda in the Arabian Peninsula, Al Qaeda in Iraq, and Al Qaeda in the Islamic Maghreb.

As Andy Liepman of the RAND Corporation cogently explained in a recent article, this development is subject to two different interpretations. While some commentators diagnose al-Qaeda as being in its final death throes, others see this franchising process as evidence that al-Qaeda is "coming back with a vengeance as the new jihadi hydra." As is often the case, the truth likely falls somewhere between these polar prognostications. Al Qaeda Core is surely weakened, but its nodes around the world have picked up the terrorist mantle and continue to pose a threat to America and its allies—as tragically evidenced by the recent violent takeover of the gas facility in Algeria and the American deaths at the U.S. mission in Benghazi last September. This threat has been compounded by a number of other variables, including the opportunities created for al-Qaeda by the events following the Arab Spring; the ongoing threat posed by Hezbollah, its confederates in Iran and other terrorist groups; and the growing incidence over the past few years of home-grown violent extremism within the United States, such as the unsuccessful plots targeting Times Square and the New York subway.

We are now at a pivot point where we need to reevaluate the means and objectives of our counterterrorism program in light of the evolving threat. The executive branch is currently engaged in that process and has undertaken a number of policy shifts to reflect the altered threat landscape. First, it is working to develop stronger cooperative relationships with governments in countries like Yemen where the al-Qaeda franchises are operating. Second, they are coordinating with other foreign partners—like the French in Mali and the African Union Mission in Somalia—who are actively working to suppress these new movements. Finally, they are building infrastructure—like the reported construction of a drone base in Niger—that will facilitate counterterrorism operations in the regions where these franchises operate.

While it is important that the administration is undergoing this strategic reevaluation, it is also important that Congress participate in that process. Over the past 12 years, Congress has made significant contributions to the post-9/11 reorientation of our counterterrorism program. First, it has been instrumental in strengthening our counterterrorism capabilities. From the Authorization for Use of Military Force passed within days of 9/11 to the Patriot Act and its reauthorization to the critical 2008 amendments to the Foreign Intelligence Surveillance Act, Congress has repeatedly answered the government's call for strong but measured authorities to fight the terrorist adversary.

Second, congressional action has gone a long way toward institutionalizing measures that were hastily adopted after 9/11 and creating a lasting framework for what will be a "long war" against international terrorism. Some argue against such legislative permanence, citing the hope that today's terrorists will go the way of the radical terrorists of the 1970s and largely fade from the scene over time. That, I'm afraid, is a pipe dream. The reality is that international terrorism will remain a potent force for years and possibly generations to come. Recognizing this reality, both Presidents Bush and Obama have made a concerted effort to look beyond the threats of the day and to focus on regularizing and institutionalizing our counterterrorism measures for the future—as most recently evidenced by the administration's effort to develop lasting procedures and rules of engagement for the use of drone strikes.

Finally, congressional action has provided one other very important element to our counterterrorism initiatives—a measure of political legitimacy that could never be achieved through unilateral executive action. At several important junctures since 9/11, Congress has undertaken to carefully consider and pass legislation in sensitive areas of executive action, such as the legislation authorizing and governing the Military Commissions and the amendments to our Foreign Intelligence Surveillance Act. On each such occasion, Congress' action had the effect of calming public concerns and providing a level of political legitimacy to the executive branch's counterterrorism efforts. That legitimizing effect—and its continuation through meaningful oversight—is critical to maintaining the public's confidence in the means and methods our government uses in its fight against international terrorism. It also provides assurance to our foreign partners and thereby encourages them to engage in the operational cooperation that is so critical to the success of our combined efforts against international terrorism.

These post-9/11 examples speak to the value that congressional involvement can bring both to the national dialogue about counterterrorism matters and specifically to the current reassessment of our strategies and policies in light of the evolving threat. It is heartening to see that Congress is starting to ratchet up its engagement in this area. For example, certain Members are expressing views about our existing targeting and detention authorities and whether they should be revised in light of the new threat picture. Some have asked whether Congress should pass legislation governing the executive branch's selection of targets for its drone program. Some have suggested that Congress establish a judicial process by which a court reviews and approves any plan for a lethal strike against a U.S. citizen before that plan is put into action. Some have proposed legislation more clearly directing the Executive branch to send terrorist suspects to military custody, as opposed to the criminal justice system. Others have argued more generally that the AUMF should be amended to account for the new threat emanating from Ansar al-Sharia, Boko Haram, and the other dangerous groups that have little direct connection to al-Qaeda and its affiliates or to anyone who ''planned, authorized, committed or aided the terrorist attacks that occurred on September 11, 2001.'' While these ideas have varying strengths and weaknesses, they are a welcome sign that Congress is poised to get substantially engaged in counterterrorism matters once again.

In assessing these and other proposals for national security legislation, Congress should be guided by a pair of principles that their legislative efforts have largely followed over the past 12 years. First, it is important to remember the practical concern that time is of the essence in counterterrorism operations and that legal authorities must be crafted in a way that permits operators and decisionmakers in the executive branch to react to circumstances without undue delay. That concern was not sufficiently appreciated prior to 9/11, and as a result many of our counterterrorism tools were burdened with unnecessary limitations and a stifling amount of process. In fact, the tools used by our national security investigators who were trying to prevent terrorist attacks were much less user-friendly than those available to criminal investigators who were investigating completed criminal acts. The result was slowed investigations and an inability to develop real-time intelligence about terrorist threats, like the one that hit home on 9/11.

The Patriot Act and subsequent national security legislation helped to rectify that imbalance and to make our counterterrorism tools and investigations more nimble and effective, while at the same time providing for sufficient safeguards and oversight to ensure that they are used responsibly and consistent with our respect for privacy and civil liberties. Any future legislation should follow that model. For instance, any scheme for regulating the use of targeted drone strikes—which may well raise myriad practical and constitutional issues beyond the concern with operational delay—should be designed with an appreciation for the need for quick decision-making and action in the context of war and targeting.

Second and more generally, Congress should maintain its record of largely resisting legislation that unduly restricts the government's flexibility in the fight against international terrorism. For example, there have been occasional efforts to categorically limit the executive branch's options in its detention and prosecution of terrorist suspects. While there may well be good principled arguments behind these efforts, pragmatism dictates that we should not start taking options off the table. We should instead maximize the range of available options and allow our counterterrorism professionals to select the mode of detention or prosecution that best serves the objectives for each particular suspect—development of intelligence, certainty of successful prosecution, etc.

Flexibility should also be the watchword when approaching any effort to amend the Authorization for Use of Military Force. The diffusion of terrorist threats that has led to the call for amending the AUMF is bound to continue, and new groups will likely be forming and mounting a threat to the United States in the years to come. Any amended AUMF must be crafted with language that clearly defines the target of our military force, but that also encompasses all such groups that pose a serious threat to our national security.

Congress is to be commended for having largely followed these principles in its legislative efforts over the past 12 years and for playing a vitally important role in the construction of our national counterterrorism program since 9/11—a role that it should continue to play in the years to come.

This committee is specifically to be commended for recognizing the recent evolution of the terrorist threat and the need to assess our counterterrorism program and policies in light of that evolution. It has been an honor to be a part of that effort, and I will be happy to answer any questions you may have.

The CHAIRMAN. Well, thank you all for your insights.

And I see we have had several colleagues join us.

So, let me start off with exploring some of what you have suggested a little greater in depth.

Most of the government's most critical counterterrorism effort takes place at the strategic level, from countering violent extremism programs to the Global Counterterrorism Forum. Have we done enough, though, to target the recruitment pipeline? And how can we enhance our efforts to undercut—I think it goes to Congresswoman Harman's comments—the extremist narrative and address the grievances that are the underlying fuel instability? Any thoughts on that?

Ms. HARMAN. Well—by the way, it is a great personal pleasure to see "Senator" Murphy. I have not called him that yet, so—a former colleague.

That is what I was really talking about. We have to win the argument with this pipeline of potential recruits. And we cannot win the argument if all we are doing is playing "Whac-a-Mole," as I call it, knocking off some folks, whom we should either apprehend or kill, depending on what the options are. Obviously, capturing is a better option, I think, when it is possible. But, nonetheless, if that is all we are perceived to do, if we have a drone-centric foreign policy, I do not think that wins the argument.

And therefore, both Mike and Ken have suggested things that we can do. I think we should put a strict legal framework around the use of drones. Congress should do this. I have recommended that we could bring drones under the FISA framework, which most in Congress supported, including then-Senator Obama. And these FISA courts, I—although some disagree—I think can work to improve the framework for the use of drones—not the operations, but the framework. And Congress can provide oversight. That is just one example of how we could win the argument with potential recruits, because then we have a rules-based program for the use of force against certain high-value targets.

The CHAIRMAN. Yes.

Mr. LEITER. Mr. Chairman——

The CHAIRMAN. And maybe—I invite your answers, but let me specify my question a little bit more. It seems that having a framework for the use of drones, assuming you give the flexibility necessary that was referred to here, may be desirable, but, at the end of the day, we do not win hearts and minds because we have a rule framework about how we might strike at somebody. We win hearts and minds because we change—or, we work to change the realities of their lives on the ground.

I mean, the Arab Spring, in my mind, is a challenge of a very young population, mostly in or near poverty, having no future—the aspirations for the future not on the horizon with any possibility of that future——

Ms. HARMAN. Yes.

The CHAIRMAN [continuing]. Being better, and then having that despair being manipulated against—whether it be the West or Israel or others.

So, should not our policy consider—and this might be a longer term context, but, nonetheless, we are in this for—despite fatigue, we are in this for a while, it certainly seems to me—aren't there other things that we should be considering?

Ms. HARMAN. Yes.

The CHAIRMAN. Yes.

Mr. LEITER. Mr. Chairman, in my view, this has been—and this is a self-indictment, since I was in both administrations, and we did not effectively do this, in my view—countering violent extremism, that ideological fight, has been woefully, in my view, underfunded and under-focused-on, compared to the kinetic piece. Now, there are a variety of reasons for this. It is really easier to get funding for weapon systems that are built in people's districts than it is to build up a mini-army of people who are going to work the Web and get our message out there, and counter al-Qaeda's message from the basement of the State Department. It is much easier to see tangible results from a kinetic strike, using a drone or anything else, than it is to understand, you know, a 1-point or a 2-point change in perceptions in the United States, as opposed to bin Laden. That is a much longer program, which requires much greater patience.

So, in my view, we can do a couple of things on this front. First of all, I do think, again, we have significantly underfunded ideological efforts at the State Department; to some extent the Department of Homeland Security; and the people who actually have the most money to do these sorts of programs, the Department of Defense. Now, with all respect to my Defense colleagues, they tend to be the worst people to actually carry the message that the United States is not at war with Islam, because they are wearing uniforms. So, we have to reallocate funds to the people who can responsibly go out and take this message.

Second, this is about acts and not just words, so we have to maintain foreign-aid programs and rule-of-law programs that are now going to help work with these emerging democracies, which we hope are democracies. And we have to work closely with them even if some of their views are very much in tension with some of our interests. These are two quick things that I would offer.

I do think that there is something heartening, also, about the Arab Awakening, though, Mr. Chairman. And I would offer that, frankly, al-Qaeda's message did not drive the Arab Awakening. Al-Qaeda was largely irrelevant to the Arab Awakening, and it is exactly the motivation that you identify, as opposed to a purely al-Qaeda-driven: we must get rid of the old regimes and move in through violence. The Arab Awakening proved that you can do this without violence. And, in that sense, we actually have an opportunity, now, going forward; although we have lost partners and we have lost some counterterrorism kinetic capability, this was actually a win for us, ideologically.

Mr. WAINSTEIN. Mr. Chairman, if I could just follow up on that last—Mike's last point.

I think the challenge was clear, from the beginning of the Arab Spring, that there is going to be a bit of a tradeoff for the United States. In the short term—if you are looking at the Arab Spring just through the counterterrorism lens—in the short term we were going to lose partners who had been reliable in the efforts against terrorism. And we have seen that. We have certainly lost some partnerships. We have lost some cooperation that we used to be able to rely on in that part of the world, a very volatile part of the world. But, the long-term solution for terrorism is not just, you know, stamping out the fires, day by day, it is to change the circumstances under which people live in that area. And the Arab Spring was a way to do that as a source of hope for democracy and economic development; and it was very important that the United States was seen on the side of the people who were looking for reform.

The additional danger, as Mike pointed out, though, is, al-Qaeda now is getting a foothold in some parts of the Arab Spring; whereas, they were completely irrelevant to the beginning of it. And so, it is all the more important that we solidify whatever cooperative relationships that we can before al-Qaeda gets more of a foothold.

The CHAIRMAN. You know, it seems to me that one of our—and I will turn to Senator Corker next—it seems to me that one of our challenges, as we think about this, whether it is the rules of engagement, the question of Congress revisiting the authorization of under what set of circumstances we use force—but, one of the key questions that we seem to sweep under the rug, which is the whole question that I was trying to get to you, I think several of you alluded to, which is that there is an underpinning here, of people's economic circumstances. And unless we deal, whether through partnership with others—and that is why I would be interested, when I come back, after the other colleagues get their chance here to question you—about what partnerships really work and how we could foster partnerships that look at, for example, development assistance. We have a challenge here on foreign aid, in general, even though it is, approximately 1 percent of the Federal budget, it is one of the most powerful tools that we have, especially when I look at this universe. You are just not going to do this by striking at individuals, which I agree, those who, in fact, are of great threat to the country and you can capture, because if you could capture them, you would want to capture them for the information flow that comes from that then you have to strike at them, but in the longer term, the changing of the dynamics here comes from how we engage in changing people's lives. And we cannot do that alone, but we certainly could engage in partnerships to do that. And the messages that flow from that are pretty dramatic, I think.

And it is something I would like to explore, because we are going to be having some challenges as we look at our budget and we look forward—and, as you said, we are not going to have $100 billion in counterterrorism money, moving forward, in the foreseeable continuous future. So, then the question is, How do we change the dynamics? How do we get better bang for our buck? And how do we change the underpinnings? That is what I am looking to get at.

With that, Senator Corker.

Senator CORKER. Thank you, Mr. Chairman.

The CHAIRMAN. Senator Murphy, if you would take over the chair while I——

Senator CORKER. He is moving from Senator to chairman awfully quickly, but—it is an amazing thing. So—yes. [Laughter.]

So, again, thank you for your testimony. And I appreciate all the comments regarding some of the softer pieces, if you will, that need to be pursued. And I agree that those certainly have not been pursued in the way they should.

And I want to go back to the legal case first. And I think each of you have said, look, al-Qaeda is more amorphous and, you know, spread around. Core al-Qaeda's been, basically—I will use some-body else's word—''decimated.'' But, it also makes it—does it not?—much more difficult to tie the groups that we are actually pursuing today back to 9/11, which is what generated the authorization for the use of military force on September 18. I think all of you would agree, it is very difficult to tie these groups back to that authorization. Is that correct?

Mr. LEITER. Yes.

Ms. HARMAN. Yes. And I would add that, those of us who voted for it—I certainly did; everyone except for one Member of Congress voted for it, as I recall—thought it would be limited in time and space. I never imagined that it would still be in force over a decade later and would be used by the executive branch to underpin a huge variety of actions against disparate enemies. That does not mean that there should not be a legal framework. I think there should be a legal framework. But, maybe one that is more attuned to the new threats, and also the goal of, I would say, Senator Corker—the goal of winning the argument, not just ''whacking'' people. That is our challenge now. And unless we can win the argument, there will be more and more people in more and more countries who are able to produce propaganda tools to recruit more and more people.

And so, that is why I said, in my testimony, that we need a whole-of-government approach to counterterrorism, which certainly includes diplomacy and development as tools. We need smarter investments. We need foreign aid budgets that do not just pick the flavor-of-the-month country, but that bear down on those countries that are the most serious threats, and perhaps condition aid based on changing some government policies. And then, we do need to live our values. And that means that everything we do should be rules-based.

Senator CORKER. So, I believe, in order for that to happen, in order for Congress and the executive branch to work together to drive that kind of effort, I really do think this entire authorization needs to be updated, and I think the debate that comes from that will cause people to look at what you are saying, and drive that. Otherwise—you know, as you mentioned, I mean, there is fatigue; people really do not want to deal with it. The executive branch is dealing with it.

And, candidly, as we travel in the field, most of the folks that we deal with, in intelligence and other places, say there is a very thin thread, if any, back to the original authorization. And I think all of you are agreeing with that.

So, let me just ask you, on that point, What would be—I know we have talked about the idealism issues. I know there are all kinds of things we need to do to help people understand our values and all those kinds of things. But, if you got back to the authorization of military force, what would some of the characteristics be of this one that are different from the one we put in place on September 18?

Mr. LEITER. Senator, I would, first, say that, in my view, the current AUMF is too broad, too narrow, and too vague. It is too broad, because, as Jane Harman said, we are now 12 years later, and I think a lot of people, when they voted for it, did not quite realize that it would still be applying. It is too narrow, because, honestly, by the end of my tenure in the U.S. Government, you were having to do some shoehorning to get some groups or individuals in there that posed a very clear and imminent threat to the United States into the language of the AUMF. And it is too vague, because I think it is very difficult to look at it and say, How would that apply to a group like Jabhat al-Nusra?—which the American people and this Congress should know, up front.

So, my suggestion would be that you have some—first of all, I would commend the Hoover Institution report on the AUMF, on reforming the AUMF. I think it is quite good. I don't agree with every word of it. I think it is a good theoretical way of considering what has to be changed.

In my view, there should be some process, somewhat similar to the designation of terrorist groups, that happens through the State Department now, where groups are nominated by the executive branch, they are approved by the executive branch, then there is some period for the U.S. Congress to review whether that group should be included in a new authorization of military force. And I would say that should include groups that pose a near-term threat to the United States through acts of terrorism. And that is going to be broader than al-Qaeda affiliates, but it will also give the Congress some opportunity to, not necessarily vote, but to at least review executive branch determinations of the types of groups that the executive branch thinks should be targeted. That is how I would approach it.

Senator CORKER. Kenneth.

Mr. WAINSTEIN. Senator, I subscribe to the idea of having a list, and the Executive can then propose that additional groups be put on that list as those groups become a serious threat to the United States. And that was one of the points I made in my initial remarks, that it needs to be a system that is flexible enough to account for the changing situation, because the threat picture today is going to be very different a year from now, and radically different 10 years from now. So, I think something along the lines of what Mike just described would be perfect.

Let me just sort of go up to 30,000 feet for a second. There are a couple of benefits to Congress considering this, at this time or any time. First, by looking at possibly revising the AUMF, it will be a recognition of what I think many of us have known for years, which is, this effort against terrorism is a long-term war. It is going to be around for a long time. This is not a threat that is going to go away once we destroy core al-Qaeda. It is going to extend well beyond 9/11 and the years since 9/11. So, it will be sort of a national recognition that we need to account for the fact that this is going to be a permanent state of life.

Also, as I mentioned in my initial remarks, right now the administration seems to be able to shoehorn their activities into the AUMF, and what they have done seems to have been covered by the law. But, there really is an element of Congress lending legitimacy to their actions when Congress deliberates over the authority that it is considering giving to the executive branch, looks at all the implications of it and vests that authority in the execu-

23

tive branch. I think it is good for all branches, and I think it would be good for our counterterrorism program.

Ms. HARMAN. Could I just raise one caution? Because I was thinking about this as both Mike and Ken were talking.

I am not sure Congress should give a blanket authorization for the use of force. I think Congress' role is to consider carefully different circumstances around different assertions of the use of force. And I do not mean that every 2 days, Congress has to consider some terrorist organization that we have not heard of before, and authorize the government to do something specifically there. But, Congress' role in oversight and legislating has to be much more assertive than it has been, in my view, over the last 12 years. And one size does not fit all. That is one point.

The second point is, calling this the ''war on terror,'' as many have, I think has not helped us win the argument. Terror is a tactic. How do you fight a war against a tactic? That was modified by the Obama administration to say it was a ''war on al-Qaeda and affiliates.'' I thought that was an improvement. But, again, I think we should be careful with our language. And perhaps this committee, the Foreign Relations Committee, that does do positive-sum things—passes a foreign aid budget, helps us project diplomacy, not just kinetic power in the world—should consider some form of authorization or some process for oversight that weighs other factors in addition to the use of force.

Senator CORKER. Well, I could not agree more. And again, I think a real debate about how broad, how narrow, how vague, how blanket an authorization is, I think will drive us to focus on all these things, which we have not been focusing on. So, I could not agree more. And I think the administration—I do not know where they are. I mean, on one hand, they are able to do whatever it is they wish; and many people in Congress like that, because they have no ownership over the outcome. But, I do think that, you know, there is almost no thread of tieback to where we were. I think it is time to update this and to create another authorization that is different. And I do think we should take some ownership over this and, hopefully, drive a little bit different approach to how we deal with this.

This is long term, you are exactly right. There is not going to be a finite end. And I think this whole debate would help invigorate the approach, and actually overcome the fatigue that we are talking about. It still is a threat, we still have issues of nation-states that we have to deal with. And obviously that is a whole nother component. But, this is one that certainly we need to be paying attention to for a long, long time.

And I thank you for your testimony.

Senator MURPHY [presiding]. Thank you, Senator Corker.

I will take it as no coincidence that Congresswoman Harman showed up and I got elevated to chairman, so I appreciate your bumping me up.

I want to fit in two questions, one on winning the argument and one on Syria.

Congresswoman Harman, you talked about working with actions, not just words. Or it actually may have been Mr. Leiter. And I have a question about how actions that we take here in the United

States are viewed abroad, and to what extent they factor into the recruitment tools.

After September 11, there was, frankly, a remarkable restraint showed in this country, in terms of anti-Islamic and Islamic-phobic—Islamophobe behavior. That worm has turned in the last 8 years, and whether it is State legislators looking at bans on shariah law or mosques being ridden out of neighborhoods or advertisers pulling their money from shows about Muslim families in the last 5 to 10 years, we have seen a remarkable increase in some pretty bad behavior toward the Islamic religion here in this country.

And I guess my question—and I will direct it to you first, Congresswoman Harman—is, How much does this matter? How much does this matter, when set against the other drivers of recruitment, whether it be our drone policy, our military policy, or economic factors within these regions? How much should we be paying attention to this turn that's happened in the United States, I would argue, in the last 5 years or so, as a means toward trying to ultimately win this argument across the globe?

Ms. HARMAN. Well, Chairman Murphy—has a nice ring—it matters a lot. I actually think our record is mixed. There are some good stories, too. Let us remember that, shortly after 9/11, a Sikh, not a Muslim, I think, gas station attendant was murdered by a mob just because he looked like he might have been Muslim, or that was what the folks who murdered him thought; and it was a black eye for America, that that happened. And there have been some very bad actions.

On the other hand, I know quite a bit about Los Angeles, where I am from and where my congressional district was, and the police department there, and the sheriff's office, have made major efforts to reach out for Muslim communities and to have advisory task forces and so forth, both to project a friendly image, but also, it is very smart policing, because if you build trust in a community, they are more likely to come forward and identify some of these folks who have clean records but who are contemplating some very bad deeds.

And, in fact, if I remember this, right in Virginia, there were five guys, who moved to Pakistan, who were plotting against America, and they were identified by their own community. These were kids, college-age or high-school-age kids, who were basically identified by their own communities so they could be apprehended, stopped.

So, it is a big part of the counterterrorism—of a good counterterrorism strategy to project tolerance and build positive relationships with a community that 99 percent of which is peace-loving and patriotic Americans. And those are the folks in the United States, and it is true around the world, too.

And one other fact to point out, and that is that more Muslims have been the target of terror attacks by al-Qaeda and affiliates than have non-Muslims. So, hopefully, the community itself—again, if we project the kind of relationship we should—will push against its own bad apples. That is a big part of the solution here.

Senator MURPHY. Any thoughts from——

Mr. LEITER. I guess I call you Senator or Half-Chairman at this point, Senator Murphy. [Laughter.]

Senator MURPHY. Same thing.

Mr. LEITER. At some risk, I am going to disagree with my friend Jane Harman. I, frankly, think that these are bricks in a wall, and the wall is the narrative that the United States is at war with Islam. And if the United States—if there was a lack of Islamophobia in the United States, al-Qaeda would still attack the United States, without a doubt. They are factors, but they are not driving, and I do not think they are dispositive factors.

The piece that I think is most important about this, besides the fact that, from my perspective, it is abhorrent and un-American and, you know, horrible that we would judge anyone by their religion in this country—the piece that I do think is important is, it undermines the willingness, in many cases, of the American Muslim community, which is the single most important community to messaging to the rest of the Muslim world that the United States is not at war with Islam—it makes it less likely that they are really going to be motivated to help and be a part of this fight. You know, despite all the Islamophobia, they are.

And I adamantly reject the view that the American Muslim community has not spoken out against al-Qaeda. The American Muslim community that does that does not get a lot of press time, but I have worked with Muslims for the past 8 years who are adamantly against them.

But, when they see Islamophobia, they are less likely to stand up and say, ''America is a great place to be, and the United States is not at war with Islam.'' And that is an important set of messengers that we can either embrace or chase away.

Senator MURPHY. Mr. Wainstein, if I could just turn to my second question, regarding Syria, which is connected to your comment about some of the optimism that comes out of the Arab Spring, in that, (a) anti-Americanism was not necessarily a driver of those revolutions, and (b) we were largely seen as being on the right side of those conflicts. What are the lessons, then, that we draw to the current conflict in Syria? Certainly, a lot of concern has been expressed, in this body, about whether or not, when Assad falls, we will be perceived on the right side, and what consequences that ultimately has for the very bad actors affiliated with extremist groups to hold sway in a democratic or semidemocratic process that plays out once Assad is gone.

Mr. WAINSTEIN. Senator, that is a very good question. And, in many ways, Syria is sort of the perfect storm, because it has developed into this civil war of horrific proportions, a human tragedy on a major scale. And then you throw in the prospects that it is now also the launching pad for a rejuvenated al-Qaeda presence in that part of the world, and, you know, it is the perfect conditions for al-Qaeda.

Obviously, you know, we have—as a matter of foreign policy—we have every reason to see the Assad regime get ushered out, but we also want to make sure that what comes in after he leaves, or is kicked out, is something that is hostile to al-Qaeda and is accommodating to our interests.

I know it is a balancing act, and the administration is in a tough position because they are trying to sort of keep al-Qaeda suppressed, but, at the same time, try to help the opposition, which, in many ways, is indistinguishable from al-Qaeda, in certain quarters.

So, I think that it is a tough one to draw lessons from, because it is the perfect storm.

Senator MURPHY. But, would you agree, today, that we are not perceived to be on the right side of this, and the danger is, is that if circumstances change and Assad goes, in the next several weeks or months, that, unless our disposition changes, that we are not really balancing that question very well right now?

Mr. WAINSTEIN. Right. You can see where we have been with other countries. Just take Libya and our decisions as to how and when to get involved, and how much to be involved, and how that was calibrated, and how that turned out. I think, in Syria right now, if Assad were to walk out, there would be a large percentage of the incoming government who would think that we were not there for them. And so, if they are looking for support, they would be less likely to look to us and more likely to look to other regimes that are less friendly.

Senator MURPHY. Thank you, Mr. Chairman.

The CHAIRMAN [presiding]. Senator Kaine.

Senator KAINE. Thank you, Mr. Chair.

I am intrigued with the winning-the-narrative argument that the Chairman raised and, Congresswoman Harman, that you raised in your testimony. And I am thinking of the winning-the-narrative argument in a slightly different way. So, one way to do it is to be truer to our principles and portray the right values to the world, and to do it in such a way that our own Muslim-American population feels like they can communicate the message. But, another thought that I have is a narrative does not have to be won by us, it can be won by other nations and other actors, globally, that can offer a countermodel to terrorism as a path to success.

And so, although this is not my area of the world, I would say, you know, a Turkey, that is a cochair with United States in the global counterterrorism forum, that has a growing GDP, that is a nation, you know, that is in the Muslim world, but that has a strong, kind of, economic track record now, that, on the sectarian-to-secular scale, is a little more over to the secular side than many; or a Morocco, with a constitutional monarchy, where the king is a lineal descendant of Mohammad, again with some tradition of respect for religious liberty, but strong—obviously, a strong Muslim nation, and an economy that has been stronger than some others— you know, helping our allies, you know, elevate their posture so that there is an alternative success model for young populations that are prone to be recruited into terrorism, that a success model is, you know, a functioning—more or less functioning government and a path to economic success.

So, some of the winning-the-narrative is not just about us, but I think some of the winning-the-narrative is about nations that many in these countries might feel more immediately akin to than us in helping them tell their stories. And I am just intrigued by that, especially, I guess, as a result of Turkey's role in cochairing this global counterterrorism forum with the United States. And I would just be interested in your thoughts on that.

Ms. HARMAN. Well, I strongly agree with you, and I think there is a big opportunity right now, especially given a reasonably close relationship between President Obama and Prime Minister Erdogan, of Turkey, to work together in partnership to do more, together, to frame a narrative and show a model to other parts of the region.

That is not to say that some of the recent actions of Turkey have been attractive. The anti-Israel and anti-Semitic rhetoric is horrible, and I think we have to condemn it. But, by and large, Turkey offers a more moderate model of an Islamist society.

Islamist political parties are not necessarily bad. I think it is much better to have these religious parties inside the tent than trying to blow up the tent, which is the al-Qaeda model. So, I am for that. But, I do agree that there are some models better than others.

And final comment on the Arab Awakening, because—we have talked about that. And certainly, the aspirations of the people who overthrew their government are enormously impressive, and their personal courage is impressive. But, some of these governments— new governments—have yet to succeed in a way that reflects democratic pluralism or tolerance. And that is very worrisome. Which is another reason why better models should be out.

So, you know, I strongly favor collaboration with Turkey to do this, and think you have a great idea.

Senator KAINE. Additional thoughts on that?

Mr. LEITER. Senator, I think you can look across and outside the region throughout the Muslim world for some really good examples. The United States partnership with Indonesia has been fantastic. And you may remember, in 2001–2002, people talked about how Indonesia could be the next Afghanistan, next home of al-Qaeda. And it simply has not. And why? Because the Indonesians have taken this seriously because of significant foreign aid, good intelligence, and good defense partnerships. Real success story.

I think the transition that Jordan is going through, slowly moving toward greater democratization in that region, in the heart of a region that has been affected by al-Qaeda—a very, very important example.

I absolutely agree with Jane Harman, as well, that, in places like Libya and Egypt, two very different challenges, we have to use our foreign aid in ways that makes them walk the right path, but we also have to take a very sophisticated look at the pressures they are under and who are in these governments. And we cannot simply look and say, ''Oh, they are a member of *x* group. We cannot work with them on anything.'' If we do that, we will cut off our nose to spite our face.

Senator KAINE. Well, one additional question, a kind of a separate topic. I am on Armed Services, as well, and we have been having a series of briefings by commanders in different AORs— AFRICOM and Southern Command—talking a lot about things like the drug trade—really, criminal networks from South America to North America, or across the Atlantic into Africa and then up to Europe. And it always strikes me, as we are talking about these criminal networks, if it is easy to move drugs, if it is easy to do human trafficking, if it is easy to move arms, if it is easy to move cash, it would be easy to move, you know, nuclear materiel or something else that could cause a significant challenge. And so, it strikes me that part of our counterterrorism challenge is the disruption of criminal networks that are not, in and of themselves, part of the same group of people that are terrorists, but that are now getting so blended together, or at least have a financial interest in working with people who have terrorism as a motive. And the more hearings I go to, the more nervous I get.

Mr. LEITER. Senator, I actually just spent 2 hours, before this, with staff from Senator Rockefeller's office and Senator Reid's office, talking about illicit networks, and you are absolutely right that it is simply the movement of people, materials, and, to some extent, ideology and money, and it is all the same networks. And especially as we have seen in North Africa, the Tuaregs and what they have enabled. It was 5 years ago; it was drugs and other things. And now it is weapons, Libya, and the like.

So, we have to get better at those networks. Those networks require not just traditional military force, which is in this region, but requires real enabling by us, in terms of aid and significant training on the Customs front, Department of Homeland Security, law enforcement, DEA. We have to look at this in a more holistic way than we have in the past.

Ms. HARMAN. That is why——

Mr. LEITER. Thank you.

Ms. HARMAN [continuing]. I just—if I might add something——

Senator KAINE. Yes.

Ms. HARMAN [continuing]. I advocated a whole-of-government approach to counterterrorism. If you just stay in silos and think, ''What can the State Department do?'' or, ''What can the Homeland Security Department do?'' you are not going to get at this problem. You have to put all the pieces together and remember that instead of a top-down structure that we saw on 9/11, now we have a horizontal structure of loosely affiliated groups, and some of them are criminal networks, and they are parasitic. They attach to each other for the purpose of funding an operation or moving goods, and then they disconnect. And we really have to see all of this as linked, and we have to think about how it will evolve. It won't look this way in 3 months or a year.

And they use the most modern technology. We should not assume that we are better digital natives than they are. These are the kids in the cafes who are inventing, I think, state-of-the-art cyber attacks and other things. And if you ask, What should we worry about at 3 a.m.? We should worry about these kids and what they are up to.

Senator KAINE. Thank you.

And thank you, Mr. Chairman.

The CHAIRMAN. Thank you.

One last set of questions, because you have been so gracious with your time. The whole question of ''drain the swamp.'' What do you envision—and I invite any of you and, Jane, you specifically mentioned it—but, what do you envision as the elements that you would promote to ''drain the swamp''?

And, second, what are the partnerships that have particularly worked well or the partnerships that we have not engaged in yet but that we should be engaging in toward this goal?

Any of you want to—it is a ladies-first——

Ms. HARMAN. All right. Well, I think we have talked about a number of them already. You know, "draining the swamp." I said whole-of-government approach, looking at foreign aid not as a flavor of the month, making sure that some of these programs in the State Department are considered in a broader context, which is, Do they really help our CT capability, or not?

But, I think some other things that were raised—partnerships with other countries; and this is the other piece that no one has discussed yet, and that is public/private partnerships. The private sector has many tools that—and a lot of agility that the public sector does not have. And especially if you look at create—I would not say "changing"—inventing education systems and models that fit some of these countries. Illiteracy is a huge terrorism recruitment tool. If people do not have any hope that they can change their circumstance, they can be more easily recruited. They also cannot get employed if they lack basic skills.

So, I think there are approaches to this that the private sector, in particular, has, and the NGO community, that we should lash onto, that would magnify, geometrically, our capability.

Mr. LEITER. Senator, I would offer, first, on the words front. Domestically, we have to do a better job of actually engaging the American Muslim community in this. The U.S. Government is pretty darn bad at this. Different elements of the government are OK at it. The FBI has some skills at it. The DHS has some skills. But, overall, we have not effectively engaged the American Muslim community.

Second, we have to accept that what the United States says about Islam on a global basis is generally dismissed. We are not a credible speaker on this subject. So, what we ought to seek to do, following on what Jane said, is, we ought to seek to empower moderate voices, rather than be the amplifier, ourselves. We have to provide funding so people can understand, so American Muslim groups and other Muslim groups around the world who counter al-Qaeda's message know how to use the Web and can actually counter al-Awlaki's message, or inspire his message more effectively, and they know how to use those tools. If it comes from a U.S. Government speaker, it probably is not going to be that effective.

On the acts front—because just the words without acts is simply hollow rhetoric—the pieces that have worked incredibly well for us in the past, disaster relief has been spectacular. If you look at the—not all the time, but what we have done in Pakistan for disaster relief and the like, Indonesia with the earthquake and tsunami—these sorts of programs, which really show a nonmilitary face, or perhaps a military face, but a military face using—doing humanitarian acts, have been incredibly effective.

Last, but not least, we should not think that we are going to win this alone. In part, we should simply be highlighting how bankrupt al-Qaeda's ideology is. If you look at the countries that have seriously rejected al-Qaeda—places like Jordan—it was not because of anything we said; it was because of al-Qaeda's acts. And we have to get better at showing how bankrupt the ideology is, how successful something like an Arab Awakening peaceful revolution can be, versus the killing of Muslims that al-Qaeda brings.

To me, those are the three main components that I would advocate for.

Mr. WAINSTEIN. Mr. Chairman, if I could just follow on Mike's comments about the domestic side. We have talked about outreach and countering radicalization here in the United States, and whether those efforts have translated into a positive message going out—emanating from the United States out to the rest of the world. Keep in mind, I think we all recognize this, but that message is also important here in the United States, as a counterterrorism matter, because we are seeing, more and more over the last few years, the phenomenon of homegrown terrorism, and we have people who are getting radicalized, here within our midst, in a way that did not happen before.

It has not happened to the degree that we saw over in Europe in the early '00s; in part, I think, because the Muslim community here in the United States—those communities generally feel a lower level of alienation than many of the communities over in Europe. But, we are starting to see an uptick over the last few years, and that is troubling.

And I believe that messaging that comes out from the United States Government—whether it is the prosecution of hate crimes or the FBI going out and doing outreach to the Muslim community—directly translates into a diminution of any interest on the part of your potential recruit to actually move up to the level of being an extremist.

And so, it has a very tangible impact on our national security here in the United States. And, the better we get at detecting the movement of terrorists around the world—and therefore, being able to interdict terrorists when they come into our country—the bigger the threat from terrorists who are here—who are ourselves. And so, that message is important.

The CHAIRMAN. Senator Corker.

Senator CORKER. I will just—one last question.

Again, I appreciate the testimony and look forward to talking to you all as we move along.

And I want to change the subject. I know you all have talked about a lot of things that I agree with, on the soft side, the message side, and in trying to deal with some of the economic issues that drive this. But, back to the authorization, and back to dealing with what we actually do, kinetically or in other ways.

As we are looking at a potential different type of authorization, do—when we deal with people kinetically—do they have to pose a direct threat to the United States? And does that threat have to be against U.S. facilities here at home, or can they be U.S. facilities abroad? Or can the United States, through—or should the United States, through an authorization like this, actually target—and I know I am using a word that you all have said we should not use—but, should we direct our activities toward people that, candidly, just disagree with our way of life, and maybe tried to hamper other Western societies? I mean, how do you—as you walk down that chain, how do you deal with an authorization in a way that really gets at the threat that we now have?

Ms. HARMAN. Carefully, is my answer. I do not think we want to trade the AUMF, which is outdated and designed for a different problem, for something that may be updated but is overly broad. I would suggest, first, that we understand what current and future threats are, and we define them carefully, if we are thinking about one statute. And I am not sure it is a good idea to think about one statute that would be the predicate for all of our actions. But, at any rate, that is where I would start.

The second point that I would make is, there should be an explicit statement that U.S. interests or U.S. persons have to be involved in order for us to target an individual. There should be no other reason to do it, unless we are in a—you know, in a ground combat or a—some kind of situation that fits the standard law-of-war definition, which this probably, presumably, would not.

Senator CORKER. But, can I just——

Ms. HARMAN. I——

Senator CORKER. Can I just—let me just ask you, on that. So, you know, I was just in Mali, and you have got three groups who have come together in northern Africa, with—by the way, with very differing reasons for being together. The Tuaregs actually have a political issue that has caused them to be a part of the conflict. It is not really, maybe, even a full insurgency, from that standpoint. But, you have—you know, it is criminality that people are dealing with there. They are, you know, a threat to Mali. They are a threat to Western thinking.

So, how would we—let us say we were in partnership, today, in a little different way, maybe more like the French are, on the ground—how would you differentiate? I mean, you know, a lot of this is just pure criminality. I mean, you've got hostage-taking, you've got drug-running. At some point, they may pose a threat. How do you deal with that?

Mr. LEITER. Senator, I would disagree a little bit with my friend Jane, in that I—first of all, I would—let me say, unequivocally— you know, you said, "Should we target people who we just disagree with?"—we should only be targeting people who pose a threat of violence.

Now the question becomes, "Violence toward whom? And how imminent must that violence be?" And, in my view, certainly violence toward the United States, our interests globally; that would be enough. It would not have to be a threat to the homeland.

Second, I do believe that we should have some authorization to use force against groups that pose a threat of violence against our allies in this fight. Because if we are talking about building up partnerships, one of the ways you build up partnerships is when your friends in x country come to you and say, "These guys are planning a terrorist attack against us now. We cannot target them. They are part of a group that has targeted you in the past, but now they are targeting us." It is very important that we can assist them with military force. So, in fact, you build that partnership up.

So, I think it should not be limited only to threats against the United States. We should have some more expansive language to use force against our close allies in this global fight.

And, in terms of imminence, I would not use language, as was used in the justification for targeting Americans—U.S. persons, American citizens, by—that was released recently—or, not released, but obtained. I think that is appropriate for targeting U.S. persons; but for non-U.S. persons, I would include a looser standard that—not "imminent," but some sort of immediacy, beyond imminence, so that, if there were historical plotting and the organization was still aligned against us, we could use military force.

But, the key is, Whom are they using force against, and how close is it? And I think, on both those, there does need to be some operational flexibility, as my friend Ken Wainstein said.

Senator CORKER. So, your friend Jane seems to be differing with you.

Ms. HARMAN. Well, I am differing. I certainly think we should prevent and disrupt plots against us around the world, and we should use appropriate means to do that. That is not always kinetic means. I think we would agree about that. But, if Congress is acting—this is why I am pausing—I think some very broad statement of U.S. interests in and aiding our allies, and so forth, will end up backfiring. I think it should be something much narrower. We do have agreements with allies, and we have section 5 of NATO, which——

Senator CORKER. Right.

Ms. HARMAN [continuing]. Is a common defense provision. And those things should stay in place. But, Congress legislating all this in one blanket statute, I would find—if the goal is to come up with a narrative that is going to persuade others to join us, I think this would not be a constructive part of that narrative.

Senator CORKER. Ken.

Mr. WAINSTEIN. If I may, Senator, just if I could follow on, on what Mike said. In terms of imminence, there has been a good bit of talk about the imminence of the threat that al-Awlaki posed at the time that he was killed, and people said, "Well, you know, he didn't have his finger on the trigger, and he wasn't about to set off a bomb." But that is not the imminence you need, whether it is an American or a non-American. He had a clear track record of targeting the United States, of fomenting and bringing recruits in to commit terrorist acts against the United States. It was clear, the threat that he posed.

But, I think it is important to recognize that, if you adopt a scheme, such as what Mike was describing—where different terrorist groups are found to be terrorist organizations and put on a list, and the government's now authorized to use military force against those organizations—then we are at war with those organizations.

And, traditionally, when you are at war against a state actor, you do not have to wait for the soldier to pull a gun out at you before you kill him. You can kill him on the battlefield, and you can kill him as he is preparing and getting poised to come out at the battlefield. So, imminence that is well back from the battlefield can justify the use of force in a war. And in this war against terrorist organizations, I think that same paradigm would apply.

Ms. HARMAN. If I could just add one more thing. I think it would—we were totally justified in the action we took against Awlaki. No question about it. There was a strong predicate there. He was inciting people to commit violent acts in the United States, and there was a long track record. And the fact that he was an American did require us to be careful in how we identified him. But, we were, and we did the right thing, in that case.

However, I think, as we go forward, saying, as Ken just did, "We are at war with a number of organizations," is a storyline that is troubling. We are trying to tell a story about America that is a positive story to persuade kids not to become suicide bombers and terrorists. And Congress has a big role in deciding how we tell that story. Yes, there should be legislative oversight and specific legislation to authorize kinetic acts. But I, again, would caution that it should deliver a message that is not just about being at war; it should deliver a message about trying to find ways to win the argument and to be at war as a last resort against those who are beyond rehabilitation.

Mr. LEITER. Senator, I know we are over time, but I just want to—I have to clarify one thing that Jane said.

Anwar al-Awlaki was not just inciting Americans, because I think there is a question whether simply being—inciting violence would be enough to be targeted. Anwar al-Awlaki was an operational commander who was actively recruiting and training bombers who were trying to blow up planes over the United States.

Ms. HARMAN. And I agree with that. I—that was—inciting people to commit violent acts was one of the things he was doing. I think we were totally justified.

And one more point that none of us has raised, which is that Congress is entitled to see the legal documents prepared by the Office of Legal Counsel in the Department of Justice, in my view, that authorize acts like the targeting of Awlaki. Some of those documents should only be seen, I think, in classified settings and by appropriate committees, but, nonetheless, it is not OK—and I think Ken said this, as well—for the executive branch to police itself. I think we have seen that movie before, and what should happen is, the separation of powers should work, and Congress should have the ability to conduct adequate oversight and to legislate.

The CHAIRMAN. Well——

Mr. WAINSTEIN. May I just respond?

The CHAIRMAN [continuing]. You will have the last word, because we are going to have to close out the hearing.

Mr. WAINSTEIN. OK. Just to respond to Congresswoman Harman's point. She makes a good point about the messaging.

When I talk about war in this context, I am just making the point that when Congress authorizes the use of military force against an organization, we are using the tools of war against an organization. Nobody should fool themselves. War is what it is, and so we draw on the traditions of war.

But, Jane makes a very good point about the messaging. And, you know, the more we talk about being at war with terrorism, the more that is misconstrued by the Muslim world, and used against us.

So, I think the terminology now from the executive branch, about ''being at war with al-Qaeda'' is dead on, because we are at war with al-Qaeda, but not with anybody who is not an adherent of al-Qaeda. I think it is important to draw that distinction, and it is important, as Jane said, just to keep mindful of the language we use, because that has real-life impacts on our relationships overseas.

The CHAIRMAN. Well, this has been incredibly helpful, and it has been insightful, and obviously there are some differences of opinion, when we get to this authorization, on what is the universe of it and what it looks like. But, it has been helpful to start that conversation.

So, again, with the thanks of the committee for all of your insights, your past service to our country, and for your forbearance today, it has been very helpful to us.

The committee's record will stand open until Friday for any members who have any questions.

And, with that, this hearing is adjourned.

[Whereupon, at 5:55 p.m., the hearing was adjourned.]

www.ingramcontent.com/pod-product-compliance
Lightning Source LLC
Chambersburg PA
CBHW080636290526
45790CB00007B/3087